First World War
and Army of Occupation
War Diary
France, Belgium and Germany

58 DIVISION
Headquarters, Branches and Services
Royal Army Ordnance Corps
Deputy Assistant Director Ordnance Services
6 October 1915 - 30 December 1915

WO95/2994/3

The Naval & Military Press Ltd
www.nmarchive.com
Published in association with The National Archives

Published by

The Naval & Military Press Ltd

Unit 10 Ridgewood Industrial Park,

Uckfield, East Sussex,

TN22 5QE England

Tel: +44 (0) 1825 749494

www.naval-military-press.com

www.nmarchive.com

This diary has been reprinted in facsimile from the original. Any imperfections are inevitably reproduced and the quality may fall short of modern type and cartographic standards.

© **Crown Copyright**
Images reproduced by permission of The National Archives, London, England, 2015.

Contents

Document type	Place/Title	Date From	Date To
Heading	WO95/2994/3		
Heading	58 Division (2/1 London Div) D.A.D.O.S. 1915 Sep-1916 Feb		
Miscellaneous	58th (London) Division, T.F., Monthly Statement In Connection With War Diaries.	02/09/1915	02/09/1915
War Diary	Ipswich	06/10/1915	02/11/1915
War Diary	Woodbridge	05/11/1915	05/11/1915
War Diary	Ipswich	10/11/1915	10/11/1915
War Diary	Framlingham	10/11/1915	10/11/1915
War Diary	Ipswich	11/11/1915	11/11/1915
War Diary	Warren Heath	12/11/1915	12/11/1915
War Diary	Ipswich	16/11/1915	17/11/1915
War Diary	Lowestoft	18/11/1915	18/11/1915
War Diary	Ipswich	22/11/1915	23/11/1915
War Diary	Lowestoft	25/11/1915	25/11/1915
War Diary	Ipswich	26/11/1915	30/12/1915

WO 95/2994/3

58 DIVISION
(2/1 London Div)

D.A.D.O.S

1915 SEP – 1916 FEB

58th (London) Division, T.F.,

Monthly statement in connection with War Diaries.

ORDNANCE SERVICES.

1. Oilskins Suits, and Sou'wester hats for Provisional Battalions have not yet been authorised by War Office. These articles are very necessary for Patrols and it is hoped that supply will soon be authorised.

2. Picks and shovels for Provisional Battalions are now being issued by Colchester.

3. Harness and vehicles, also other stores due to complete Units up to A.F./G.1099 are rapidly coming to hand.

4. Rear lamps for vehicles and cycles are not yet being supplied. These stores are very necessary to enable Units to comply with lighting regulations, and if supply cannot be made it is recommended that local purchase be approved.

Red House Park,
Ipswich.
2nd Sept. 1915.

Captain.
D.A.D.O.S.
58th (London) Division.

Army Form C. 2118.

WAR DIARY
or
INTELLIGENCE SUMMARY. D.A.D.O.S. 58 (London) Division

(Erase heading not required.)

2 sheets

Instructions regarding War Diaries and Intelligence Summaries are contained in F. S. Regs., Part II. and the Staff Manual respectively. Title pages will be prepared in manuscript.

[Stamp: 58th (LONDON) DIVISION GENERAL STAFF 3-NOV 1915]

Hour, Date, Place	Summary of Events and Information	Remarks and references to Appendices
6/10/15. France	Coloring Tentage – some tents were discovered with colouring washed out through rain. Orders given for re-colouring	
8/10/15. "	Arrival. Lieut. L. Leekie. A.O. Dept. arrived in relief of Captain J. Meager A.O.D. under orders for overseas.	
11/10/15. "	Hospital. 1. Private A.O.C. admitted to Hospital.	
12/10/15. "	Departure. Captain J. Meager A.O.D. embarked for overseas.	
14/10/15. "	Arrival. 1. Staff Sergt. A.O.C. joined for duty.	
16/10/15. "	Arrival. 1. Private A.O.C. joined for duty.	
19/10/15. "	Vehicle. 4 Carts Maltese, 22 Water Carts, and 9. limbered G.S. Wagons arrived & were issued to various units. Steps have been taken to have them marked in accordance with regulations.	
23/10/15. "	Vehicle. Unsuitable and unserviceable Civilian wagons replaced by service ones recommended to Head Qrs 1st Army, for disposal by sale.	

2nd sheet.

WAR DIARY
INTELLIGENCE SUMMARY
(Erase heading not required.)

Army Form C. 2118.

D.A.D.O.S. 58th (London) Division

Hour, Date, Place	Summary of Events and Information	Remarks and references to Appendices
27/10/15.	Finnish Horse of D.A.D.O.S. withdrawn. Rail journeys overscattered area of division leaves scanty time for office routine. Time is lost waiting for trains. Allotment of a Motor Car to be at disposal of D.A.D.O.S. is promised early next month.	
28/10/15.	Wagon Ammn. 1. Ammn. Wagon B.L. 5" howitz, still under repair at Woolwich; its return to this division has been hastened.	
28/10/15.	Ordnance B.L. 15 br. 2. Guns B.L. 15 br. still under repair at Woolwich. D.D.O. Woolwich asked to return early.	
28/10/15.	Fine Regr. A second horse-rug for horse picketed in the open approved. Violent storms, rains coming along.	
29/10/15.	Dial Sights No. 3. Four Dial sights overhauled and repaired by Armt. Artificer. Serviceable now.	
30/10/15.	Carriage B.L. 15 br. Two Carriages overhauled and repaired by Armt. Artificer. Serviceable now.	
31/10/15.	Elevating Gear. Three sets overhauled & repaired by Armt. Artificer. Serviceable now.	

F. Hickie Lt.
D.A.D.O.S. 58th (LONDON) DIVISION.

Approved
1/11/15.

Army Form C. 2118

WAR DIARY
or
INTELLIGENCE SUMMARY (4 sheets) D.A.D.O.S. 58th London Division

(Erase heading not required.)

Instructions regarding War Diaries and Intelligence Summaries are contained in F. S. Regs., Part II. and the Staff Manual respectively. Title Pages will be prepared in manuscript.

Place	Date	Hour	Summary of Events and Information	Remarks and references to Appendices
Ipswich	2nd	10 am	Boards held to condemn clothing	
Woodbridge	5"	11 am	Boards held to condemn clothing	
Ipswich	10"	10 am	Machine Guns for Divisional Unit – C.O.O. Colchester, reports not available	
Framlingham	10"	1 pm	Boards held to condemn clothing	
Ipswich	11"	2 pm	Limbered G.S. wagons urgently required for repairs, ordered to be withdrawn from Infantry Battalion, and to be replaced by L.S. wagons	
Lowestoft	12"	3 pm	Boards held to condemn clothing	
Ipswich	16"	11 am	Stoves dryers, and Aldershot Pattern Ovens, required for Central feeding furnaces for Units cooking in the open. – This service not being covered by regulations was referred to Head Quarters 1st Army for approval, reply received R.E. should construct improvised ovens, but owing to inclement weather, matter referred again for consideration, no reply to hand yet.	

Stamps: 58th (LONDON) DIVISION GENERAL STAFF 2 – DEC. 1915; CENTRAL REGISTRY – 6 DEC. 1915

1875 Wt. W593/826 1,000,000 4/15 J.B.C. & A. A.D.S.S./Forms/C. 2118.

Army Form C. 2118

WAR DIARY
or
INTELLIGENCE SUMMARY
(Erase heading not required.)

2nd phot DADOS. 58 [Division]

Instructions regarding War Diaries and Intelligence Summaries are contained in F. S. Regs., Part II. and the Staff Manual respectively. Title Pages will be prepared in manuscript.

Place	Date	Hour	Summary of Events and Information	Remarks and references to Appendices
Ipswich	17th	11 a.m.	Motor Car at disposal of DADOS' withdrawn. This handicaps proper Ordnance Supervision over 64 Units scattered over area of about 80 miles. Wastage and accumulation of stores cannot be watched, by sitting in an office & accepting written statements, because a Unit may from its own point of view consider certain articles are no longer fit for the service, but from an Ordnance point of view the case is totally different. Waiting on railway stations & retold trains to various forts interferes with time for office routine. An application for a car will be made again.	
Lowestoft	18th	6 p.m.	Japanese Rifles & Japanese Ammunition of 3 Provisional Battns to be withdrawn, and to be replaced by Japanese Carbines + Ammun.	
Ipswich	22nd	9 a.m.	Hiring of tentage for Recreation and Central Feeding to cease. Tentage should be drawn from A.O.D	
Ipswich	23rd	9 a.m.	Telephone Equipment all Coy Units complete.	

WAR DIARY
or
INTELLIGENCE SUMMARY

Army Form C. 2118

3rd Shot. 56th London Division

Place	Date	Hour	Summary of Events and Information	Remarks and references to Appendices
Lowestoft	25th	10 p.m.	1/25 Cyclist Batt. London Regt. to be held in readiness for service in E. AFRICA. No check, they are to proceed as Infantry. Arrangements made to transfer their bicycles to another unit, also certain explosives, machine guns ordered to Enfield. Service being Urgent Lieut. H. GLOVER attached to A.O.D. was sent from Ipswich to LOWESTOFT to witness the transfer.	
Ipswich	26th	9 a.m.	Complaints arising through units not being allowed picketing ropes 40 feet + 80 feet + 6 feet picket posts under the Equipment Regulations, for marking lineal lines for their animals. The matter was referred to Superior authority, and resulted in local purchase of the details being approved.	
Ipswich	27th	9 a.m.	Certain 2nd Line R.F.A. T.F. Units will shortly be equipped with 9.45. 18 pdr. guns to replace Bt. 15 pdrs. 2/2 London Brigade R.F.A. are about to be armed with 9/4.18.	
Ipswich	27th	11 a.m.	pdr. equipment	

Army Form C. 2118

WAR DIARY
or
INTELLIGENCE SUMMARY

"Sheet. DADOS' 58 (London Division)
4 (Erase heading not required.)

Place	Date	Hour	Summary of Events and Information	Remarks and references to Appendices
Ipswich	28th	9 am	One Armoured Antiques only is available for the Armoured work of the Division, steps to be taken to get 3 Wheelers & others from R.A. to assist. Light Car of 9/H.H.Y. Carriages of 1/1. Brigade R.F.a. repaired and put into a serviceable condition.	
Ipswich	29th	9 am	3 Provisional Battalions have returned the whole of their Japanese Rifles, and are being armed with Japanese Carbines.	
Ipswich	30th	1 pm	Local Expenditure during November is:- Hiring tents etc. £ 421. 12. 5 Repairs £ 142. 2. 0 Local Purchases £ 131. 14. 2 Total £ 695. 8. 7	

G. Leake Lieut-Col
A.D.D.S. 58th (LONDON) DIVISION.

Army Form C. 2118

WAR DIARY
or
INTELLIGENCE SUMMARY
(Erase heading not required.)

2 sheets   D.A.D.O.S. 58th (London) Division

Instructions regarding War Diaries and Intelligence Summaries are contained in F.S. Regs., Part II. and the Staff Manual respectively. Title Pages will be prepared in manuscript.

Place	Date	Hour	Summary of Events and Information	Remarks and references to Appendices
	1915			
Ipswich	Dec. 1st		Indents for stores previous to 1st July 1915 cancelled by WO. Celebrates — all outstanding items to be re-demanded by Units where necessary in part	58th (London Division) General Staff 2 - JAN 1916
"	8th		18 for O.E. Guns, Carriages & Limbers received & issued for the Brigades to be trained in their use	
"	9th		2/Cpl. Stevenson ACC (Clerk) joined for duty at Divnl. Hd. Qrs.	
"	11th		Instructions received that in future the 3rd & 6th Provisional Brigades will be administered for Ordnance Services by 1st Army.	
"	12th		A Divisional Workshop need for repairs to vehicles &c. for Command Artillery. Vide R.A. Orders supervision of AOC Armament Artificer work.	
			O.7.18 pr. ammn. received and issued — no further issues.	
"	15th		2/Sergt. Bartlett AOC joined to take over duties of Brigade O.O. officer reported to 173rd Brigade. Also 4 Armt. Artfrs. joined & posted to 2/1, 2/3, 2/3 & 2/4 Battersea R.F.A. respectively	
"	14th		Cpl. Green AOC joined to take over duties B. Brigade O.O. officer and posted to 174th Brigade. Also 4 clerks	

1875 Wt. W593/826 1,000,000 4/15 J.B.C. & A. A.D.S.S./Forms/C. 2118.

Army Form C. 2118

WAR DIARY
INTELLIGENCE SUMMARY

(Erase heading not required.)

Sheet 2

Staff 58th (London) Division

Place	Date	Hour	Summary of Events and Information	Remarks and references to Appendices
Ipswich	Dec. 1915 23rd		Lieut-Col Berg joined to take over duties of Chief Clerk at Hdqrs.	
"	" 25th		Return of Wagons G.S.T. reqd. to replace all other patterns with Division sent to Central Force & 1st Army.	
"	" 26th		Notification received that Machine Guns for Infantry are not yet available.	
"	" 27th		Amm. Shrapnel QF 18pr. issued to complete to 100 rounds per gun for RFA Brigades.	
"	" 28th		Pte Kendal A.S.C. (Saddler) posted to Aldershot.	
"	" 29th		Information received from Central Force that MK X Wagons will shortly be issued to replace all other patterns. Consignment list called for.	
"	" 30th		O.C. 2/2nd Brigade reported transfer B/15 pdr equipment thus completing the Bdes of the Division.	

Ipswich
31.12.15

for D.A.D.O.S. 58TH (LONDON) DIVISION.

Army Form C. 2118

WAR DIARY
INTELLIGENCE SUMMARY

D.A.D.O. 58th (London) Division
Ipswich 31/1/16

(Erase heading not required.)

Instructions regarding War Diaries and Intelligence Summaries are contained in F. S. Regs., Part II. and the Staff Manual respectively. Title Pages will be prepared in manuscript.

Place	Date	Hour	Summary of Events and Information	Remarks and references to Appendices
			Nil	

Stamp: 58th (LONDON) DIVISION — 31 JAN 1916 — GENERAL STAFF

F. Lee Kee. Lieut.
D.A.D.O. 58 (London) Division

1875 Wt. W593/826 1,000,000 4/15 J.B.C. & A. A.D.S.S./Forms/C. 2118.

Army Form C. 2118

WAR DIARY
INTELLIGENCE SUMMARY
(Erase heading not required.)

D.A.D.O.S. 58th (London) Division.

Instructions regarding War Diaries and Intelligence Summaries are contained in F. S. Regs., Part II. and the Staff Manual respectively. Title Pages will be prepared in manuscript.

Place	Date	Hour	Summary of Events and Information	Remarks and references to Appendices

February 1916.

Nil.

[Stamp: 58th (LONDON) DIVISION — 1 MAR 1916 — GENERAL STAFF]

E. Leckie. Lieut:
D.A.D.O.S. 58TH (LONDON) DIVISION.

1875 Wt. W593/826 1,000,000 4/15 J.B.C. & A. A.D.S.S./Forms/C. 2118.

www.ingramcontent.com/pod-product-compliance
Lightning Source LLC
Chambersburg PA
CBHW081515160426
43193CB00014B/2699